MY CALENDAR:
MONTHS OF THE YEAR

Luana K. Mitten

Rourke
Publishing LLC
Vero Beach, Florida 32964

www.rourkepublishing.com

PHOTO CREDITS: © José Luis Gutiérrez: Title Page; © Ekatrina Romanova, © Artproem, © Julián Rovagnati: page 3; © Kolja: page 4, 6, 8, 10, 12, 13, 14, 15, 16, 18, 19, 20; © Losevsky Pavel: page 5; © Gary Blakely: page 7; © René Baumgartner: page 9; © Gary Paul Lewis: page 11; © PhotographerOlympus: page 12; © Christine Balderas: page 13, 15; © Prohor Gabrusenoc: page 14; © Thomas Perkins: page 15; © Galyna Andrushko: page 17; © 77DZIGN: page 19; © Alan Dyck: page 21; © Kristy Pargertor, © Colin Sautar: page 22; © Andrew Dernie, © Connet Marie Ben, © YinYang, © jojo100: page 23

Editor: Kelli Hicks

Cover design by Nicola Stratford, bdpublishing.com

Interior Design by Heather Botto

Library of Congress Cataloging-in-Publication Data

Mitten, Luana K.
  My calendar : months of the year / Luana Mitten.
      p. cm. -- (Concepts)
  ISBN 978-1-60472-410-3
  1. Calendar--Juvenile literature. 2. Months--Juvenile literature. I. Title.
  CE13.M582 2009
  529'.3--dc22
                            2008024839

Printed in the USA

CG/CG

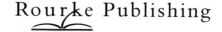

Rourke Publishing

www.rourkepublishing.com – rourke@rourkepublishing.com
Post Office Box 3328, Vero Beach, FL 32964

Twelve months
make a year!

Let's name them
one by one.

The first month starts with J and ends with Y.

JANUARY spells January.
The year is just beginning.

4

5

The second month starts with **F** and ends with **Y**.

FEBRUARY spells February.
The presidents are many.

MARCH

S	M	T	W	T	F	S
24	25	26	27	28	29	1
2	3	4	5	6	7	8
9	10	11	12	13	14	15
16	17	18	19	20	21	22
23	24	25	26	27	28	29
30	31	1	2	3	4	5

2008

The third month starts with M and ends with H.

MARCH spells March.
Say good-bye to winter.

S	M	T	W	T	F	S
30	31	1	2	3	4	5
6	7	8	9	10	11	12
13	14	15	16	17	18	19
20	21	22	23	24	25	26
27	28	29	30	1	2	3
4	5	6	7	8	9	10

2008

The fourth month starts with **A** and ends with **L**.

APRIL spells April.
Welcome springtime showers.

10

11

S	M	T	W	T	F	S
27	28	29	30	1	2	3
4	5	6	7	8	9	10
11	12	13	14	15	16	17
18	19	20	21	22	23	24
25	26	27	28	29	30	31
1	2	3	4	5	6	7

2008

Happy Mothers day

The fifth month starts with **M** and ends with **Y**.

MAY spells May.

12

The sixth month starts with J and ends with E.

S	M	T	W	T	F	S
1	2	3	4	5	6	7
8	9	10	11	12	13	14
15	16	17	18	19	20	21
22	23	24	25	26	27	28
29	30	1	2	3	4	5
6	7	8	9	10	11	12

2008

JUNE spells June. Summer comes and the year is half done!

13

M	T	W	T	F	S	S
30	1	2	3	4	5	6
7	8	9	10	11	12	13
14	15	16	17	18	19	20
21	22	23	24	25	26	27
28	29	30	31	1	2	3
4	5	6	7	8	9	10

2008

The seventh month starts with J and ends with Y.

JULY spells July.

14

The eighth month starts with **A** and ends with **T**.

S	M	T	W	T	F	S
27	28	29	30	31	1	2
3	4	5	6	7	8	9
10	11	12	13	14	15	16
17	18	19	20	21	22	23
24	25	26	27	28	29	30
31	1	2	3	4	5	76

2008

AUGUST spells August.
School's starting soon!

15

SEPTEMBER

S	M	T	W	T	F	S
31	1	2	3	4	5	6
7	8	9	10	11	12	13
14	15	16	17	18	19	20
21	22	23	24	25	26	27
28	29	30	1	2	3	4
5	6	7	8	9	10	11

2008

The ninth month starts with **S** and ends with **R**.

SEPTEMBER spells September. Fall has just begun.

16

S	M	T	W	T	F	S
28	29	30	1	2	3	4
5	6	7	8	9	10	11
12	13	14	15	16	17	18
19	20	21	22	23	24	25
26	27	28	29	30	31	1
2	3	4	5	6	7	8

2008

The tenth month starts with O and ends with R.

OCTOBER spells October.

The eleventh month
starts with **N**
and ends with **R**.

S	M	T	W	T	F	S
25	26	28	29	30	31	1
2	3	4	5	6	7	8
9	10	11	12	13	14	15
16	17	18	19	20	21	22
23	24	25	26	27	28	29
30	1	2	3	4	5	6

2008

NOVEMBER spells
November. Almost time for winter.

19

The twelfth month starts with D and ends with R.

DECEMBER spells December.
Now the year is ending...

20

21

...and a new year is beginning.

JANUARY

FEBRUARY

MARCH

APRIL

MAY

JUNE

22

JULY

AUGUST

SEPTEMBER

OCTOBER

NOVEMBER

DECEMBER

23

Index

year   3, 4, 13, 20, 22
January   4, 22
February   6, 22
March   8, 22
April   10, 22
May   12, 22
June   13, 22

July   14, 23
August   15, 23
September   16, 23
October   18, 23
November   19, 23
December   20, 23

Further Reading

Carle, Eric. *The Very Hungry Caterpillar*. Scholastic. 1994.
Rosenstiehl, Agnes. *Silly Lilly and the Four Seasons*. Raw Junior, LLC. 2008.
Ward, Cindy and de Paola, Tomie. *Cookie's Week*. Putnam. 2004.

Recommended Websites

www.ms.k12.il.us/mecc/learning.htm
www.iage.com/kidlink.html
www.fisher-price.com/us/little-people/section.asp?section=ONLINE

About the Author

Luana Mitten likes all 12 months but is especially happy in May because it's her birthday month!